UNDERSTANDING LEADERSHIP

LEARN2LEAD

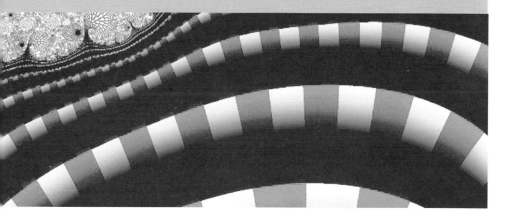

Learn2Lead
© FIEC / The Good Book Company Ltd, 2007

The Good Book Company
Elm House, 37 Elm Road, New Malden, Surrey KT3 3HB, UK
Tel: 0845-225-0880
Fax: 0845-225-0990
Email: admin@thegoodbook.co.uk
Internet: www.thegoodbook.co.uk

Unless indicated, all Scripture references are taken from the HOLY BIBLE,
NEW INTERNATIONAL VERSION. Copyright © 1973, 1978, 1984
International Bible Society. Used by permission.

ISBN 13: 978 1905564729

Printed in India

LEARN2LEAD

UNDERSTANDING LEADERSHIP

WELCOME

Welcome to the *Understanding Leadership* track of the *Learn2Lead* course – part of the local-church leadership training programme initially developed by the Fellowship of Independent Evangelical Churches. We hope you find this course both enjoyable and useful to your life and ministry.

It is likely that you will be using this book as part of a group within your congregation. But it is also possible to work through this material alone. Whichever method applies to you, we would encourage you to work prayerfully and diligently through the material, taking every opportunity to discuss the work with Christians around you.

CONTENTS

UNDERSTANDING LEADERSHIP

PREFACE

'THE THINGS YOU HAVE HEARD me say in the presence of many witnesses entrust to reliable men who will also be qualified to teach others' (2 Timothy 2:2)

Developing leaders in the church is the purpose of *Learn2Lead*. Leadership of the body of Christ is important, and therefore taking time to develop the leaders of the future is a vital aspect of building up God's church.

LEADERSHIP IS THE KEY

If you asked your Christian friends to sum up their feelings about contemporary church life, two of the words that would crop up most frequently might well be *frustration* and *disappointment*. How can that be? It's not because there's anything wrong with the gospel. That is still the power of God for the salvation of everyone who believes in the Lord Jesus Christ. It may be something to do with the way we do church. God has given us all the resources we need to fulfil his plans for this generation, but there is a crying need to discover, nurture, train and liberate the ministries of people within the church. And that means competent and effective leadership.

CHANGING THE CULTURE

Many of us come from a background where everyone expected the Minister to do everything – except perhaps play the organ, teach Sunday School or make the tea. And more disturbingly, the Minister expected it to be that way too. The vision for *Learn2Lead* is to create a culture where everyone in the church – especially young people – see leadership as something they aspire to. When Paul wrote to Timothy, he obviously expected that there would be people in the church who wanted to be leaders. We want people in the church to see their leaders at work and say, 'Under God, I'd love to be able to do that!'

WHAT IS LEARN2LEAD?

Learn2Lead is an introductory course for church members who are not in a position to take time off work for more preparation for their role as leaders. It draws on the experience of the team that already trains people through a residential and placement programme called *Prepared for Service*. When you have completed *Learn2Lead* you may consider further study under the *Prepared for Service* programme or alternatively, with the Open Bible Institute. Details of these organisations can be found at the end of this workbook.

WHO TEACHES LEARN2LEAD?

The Scriptures indicate that those who are already doing important work in the church have it as their responsibility to train others to carry forward the work. The apostle Paul told his son in the faith, Timothy, 'The things you have heard me say in the presence of many witnesses entrust to reliable men who will also be qualified to teach others' (2 Timothy 2:2).

 Learn2Lead is a tool for experienced leaders to use to teach others. It is designed to help those 'at the helm' to assist a new generation of leaders as they learn how to lead others. Tutors will normally be church leaders and others whose ministry has earned the respect and confidence of those they lead.

WHO MARKS LEARN2LEAD?

Learn2Lead is a course designed for use within your congregation under the guidance of your church leader. Their feedback is going to be the most beneficial to you as they know you as a person and see your ministry in action. However, you may also like an independent person to look at your work, mark it and (if successful) issue you with a certificate that acknowledges your many hours of study. If this is the case then you are welcome to submit a folder of your work (containing answers to each of the exercises in this book) to the Open Bible Institute. For full details (including the current marking fee) please see the website: *www.open-bible-institute.org.*

WHO IS LEARN2LEAD FOR?

It is for everyone in the local church who has the potential to be a leader. And the definition of leadership? That quality that makes other people want to follow you. You may be in leadership already as an elder or youth work co-ordinator. Perhaps people in the church have suggested that you have the leadership gifts that could be developed for the future. *Learn2Lead* is not just for potential church leaders, it is also hoped that it will assist any church member who is given responsibility in the church.

FIVE TRACKS

Learn2Lead consists of five tracks of training looking at the knowledge, skills and attitudes required to be developed by leaders in the church.

Understanding the Bible, Understanding Doctrine, Understanding Leadership, Leadership in Practice 1 and Leadership in Practice 2

THREE ELEMENTS TO THE COURSE

There are three elements to the course:

1. **Individual study** – this should be done before meeting with your tutor and the group.
2. **Group session** – this would normally include a review of individual study; discussion of some of the answers; review of any action points from the previous group session and preview of the next unit to be studied etc.
3. **Ministry opportunity** – there may be ways in which the study material from the unit can be implemented in your own ministry.

So *Learn2Lead* is not just about gathering information and getting the answers right but also applying that information so that you learn by experience in the church.

THE TOOLS YOU WILL NEED

• **Bible** – *Learn2Lead* uses the NIV Bible throughout.

• **Notebook** – You will need to make a record of your answers to questions and other notes and we suggest you have a notebook which you can use in conjunction with this student manual. At the end of these ten units, there is the option to submit the work you have done for marking by the Open Bible Institute. All students who submit work of an appropriate standard will be issued with a certificate. If you would like to work towards this certificate, please keep all your answers to the unit questions in your notebook. Once you have finished unit 10, neat versions of your answers can be submitted to the Open Bible Institute with the appropriate marking fee.

• **Bible Dictionary** – It would be useful for you to have access to a good Bible Dictionary. Student discounts are available through the Open Bible Institute office.

THE SYMBOLS

- The Bible passages by this symbol must be read. There are also a number of other references which should be looked at if you have time.

- These questions are designed to be worked through on your own and usually have factual answers.

- These questions are designed for discussion during your group meeting. Come prepared with some ideas.

- The six Old Testament units from Understanding the Bible have questions with this symbol. They are important as they show the 'big picture' of what God planned and did through Jesus Christ throughout history.

- These are points of application and further work which will help you to develop what you have learned in the unit.

The value of *Learn2Lead* is not only found in the quality of the material but particularly in its application. This is the secret of effective leadership in the body of Christ. The *Learn2Lead* team are interested in ensuring that the words contained within this book come alive in your role of leadership and in the church as a whole. If you can help us develop the material to ensure that this continues to happen please contact us, we would love to hear how you are progressing.

Remember leadership is action – never just a position!

Learn2Lead c/o The Good Book Company,
Elm House, 37 Elm Road, New Malden, Surrey KT3 3HB, UK
For further information please also see the FIEC website: www.fiec.org.uk

FACING THE CHALLENGE

THE AIM OF THIS UNIT is to get you thinking about whether God is gifting you for church leadership. What me, a leader? Why not! Paul says that if anyone sets their heart on leadership, they desire a noble task (1 Timothy 3:1). And, anyway, the Bible is full of reluctant leaders, like Moses and Gideon – men and women. So, why not you? At the very least, thinking through the challenge of leadership and seeking God's direction for your life can only be a good thing. Who knows where it will lead?

Here are some questions to get you thinking...

1. What's your image of a good leader? Write down three qualities that you look for in leaders.

2. How does inserting the word 'Christian' into the question change your view of leadership?

3. Think about someone who leads a ministry in your church. What do you particularly appreciate about them?

GET INTO THE BIBLE

Here are some case studies

 CASE STUDY I: MOSES AND JOSHUA
Read Joshua 1:1-5

For the background to the account of Joshua, see the Understanding the Bible Track, Unit 1.3.

Joshua succeeds Moses as Israel's leader. His new job? Leading more than two million people into a strange land, occupied by hostile tribes and conquering it. That's a challenge!

 What qualities does he possess to become the leader of God's people?
Check out the following references...
• Numbers 27:18-23
• Exodus 17:9-14
• Exodus 24:13
• Numbers 14:1-9

A change at the top at such a critical moment in Israel's history sounds pretty undesirable but, because Joshua has assisted Moses for many years, he is prepared to take over the leadership of the nation. This kind of seamless transition doesn't happen by chance. It demands that we take leadership as seriously as God does. Leaders need to be identifying and training others who have the potential to take their place. And those of us who aspire to leadership need to be ready to seize opportunities to learn whenever they arise.

 CASE STUDY II: DEBORAH
Read Judges 4:4-10

Deborah is unique among the judges of Israel.

 1. What qualities mark her out as a good leader?
2. Are there any hints in this passage why a woman is leading Israel?
3. Can you see any limitation on Deborah's leadership?

CASE STUDY III: PAUL AND TIMOTHY
Read 2 Timothy 3:10-4:4

Here is another dynamic duo – Paul and Timothy. Like Joshua, Timothy is more than just a convert to the faith, he has been apprenticed to the great Apostle, Paul. Apprenticeship is a brilliant way to learn. Rather than being cut off from the action and getting it all out of books in the rarefied atmosphere of college, you're actually engaged in the thick of it. You watch the experts at work, picking it up as they talk their way through what they're doing. You get to have a go yourself, under their guidance and supervision. Together, you analyse how you're getting on and you learn from your successes and mistakes. Gradually, your tutor allows you more and more freedom, until you're confident and skilful enough to do it on your own. It's called learning by experience – not being thrown in at the deep end and left to sink or swim. The master-craftsman is always available to direct. . . explain. . . advise. . . correct.

In this passage, we see how Paul has given Timothy exactly this blend of detailed instruction and hands-on pastoral experience. You can see how Timothy's apprenticeship has followed two main tracks – teaching and practical Christian living (3:10). Now, he's exercising leadership in his own right in a demanding church situation in Ephesus. And notice that little clue Paul gives us into good training in 3:14 – it's not just what you know; it's whom you've learned it from that counts.

THINK IT THROUGH

1. What do the examples of Joshua and Timothy have in common?
2. What is different about their 'call' to leadership?
3. Look at 1 Timothy 4:14. What part does the local church play in setting Timothy apart for ministry? Try to find out how he gets to join Paul's missionary team.
4. Look at the experience of the early churches planted by Paul from Acts14:21b-24. What is one of the keys to their continued growth?
5. Using a good commentary, research verse 23 to discover what you can about the way leaders are recognised in the early church.
6. What opportunities are you given to serve God in your church? Or what opportunities would you like to be given?

FOLLOW IT UP...

1. Do you have a wife, husband, fiancé or a fiancée with whom you need to share your thoughts about leadership before you go any further?
2. Under the direction of your tutor, talk to one of the leaders in your church. Tell them what you appreciate about their work and ask what they find rewarding or challenging about being a leader. Ask what gifts they see developing in your life.
3. Is there someone who could provide you with the kind of mentoring role of Moses or Paul? Pray about it and, if you want to take it further, talk to your tutor or one of your church leaders.

MEETING THE MARK

THE AIM OF THIS UNIT is to show you the qualities
God is looking for in church leaders. Imagine other people
in church are encouraging you. . . there are opportunities
for you to serve. But what qualifications do you need to
be a church leader? Someone has, rather tongue in cheek,
suggested that good leaders must have the strength of an
ox, the bounce of a kangaroo, the tenacity of a bulldog, the
perspective of a giraffe, the daring of a lion, the endurance
of a camel, the wisdom of an owl, the constitution of a
horse, the harmlessness of a dove, the disposition of an
angel, the industry of a beaver, the loyalty of an apostle, the
gentleness of a sheep, the patience of a saint, the versatility of
a chameleon, the faithfulness of a prophet, the vision of an
eagle, the fervency of an evangelist, the hide of a rhinoceros,
the devotion of a mother… and still they wouldn't please
everybody!

What qualities does God look for in a leader? Discuss in your group…

1. Which is more important – what we are for God or what we do for God? Why?
2. Leaders are able to devote part or all of their time to growing God's work. Strangely, it is a privilege fraught with dangers. What do you imagine might be some of the greatest dangers that leaders face?

GET INTO THE BIBLE

Read 1 Timothy 3:1-16

Humanly speaking, everything stands or falls with leadership. In this passage, Paul is setting out to remind Timothy of the kind of leadership he is to look for in the church at Ephesus. He is speaking specifically about elders and deacons, but the principles apply to everyone in leadership.

What kind of men does God want to be elders? Scripture lays down some pretty solid requirements. Study the lists here in 1 Timothy 3:2-7 and in Titus 1:6-9.

That's a tall order by anybody's standard. Does God beam down pre-packaged leaders from heaven? No, we have to grow them. Lots of the leaders in the Bible were tested first as servants. Joseph was a servant in Egypt for 13 years before being promoted to Prime Minister. Moses cared for sheep for 40 years before God called him. And, as we've seen already, Joshua was Moses' servant before he became Moses' successor.

We can identify three stages in preparing anyone for ministry. . .
• first we need to be tested in the general life and witness of the church
• then we need to be tempered in some specific ministry under supervision; and
• finally we can be trusted with full leadership responsibility.

Where does this holy lifestyle spring from? The last few verses of our passage (vv 14-16) hold the key. We grow holiness of life in the context of the church. The pictures Paul draws here are very instructive in the setting of this chapter. Church is…

• **God's family** – the environment in which his children grow. Here they are loved, nurtured and disciplined so that every family member realises their potential and is prepared for maturity – including future leaders

• **God's temple** – Ephesus is dominated by the temple to Diana, one of the seven wonders of the ancient world. But God is creating a greater wonder still – a temple where his name is worshipped and his values are promoted. The temple to Diana is the source of endemic social breakdown in Ephesian life, the church is the pillar and ground of the truth.

It's in this setting of family and temple that Timothy as lead-elder in the

Ephesian church is to grow the next generation of Christian leaders.

And the secret of godly living? Jesus Christ – the One who has come from heaven . . . has been vindicated by the Holy Spirit. . . who has been seen by angels but whose ministry is for us. . . the one who is preached around the world and is believed on by more people today than ever before. . . the one who is at his Father's right hand in glory and from there will come to claim back the universe for God. He is the One who gives qualified, gifted leaders to carry on the work.

 ## THINK IT THROUGH

1. How does God want to use the church family to which you belong to promote spiritual growth in your life? And how does he want to use you to promote spiritual growth in your church?

2. Scan the Bible passages used in this Unit again. What do the personnel profiles remind you of?

• the thrusting business executive determined to get to the top?

• the mature Christian, eager to serve?

Compare the similarities and the differences between these two images.

3. Which is the one gift the elder must display that is not a requirement of every mature believer?

 ## FOLLOW IT UP

1. Take an honest look in the mirror. Do you see signs of. . .

• personal integrity

• spiritual maturity

• church experience

• a well-ordered home-life?

In which area do you feel you need most help?

LIVING THE LIFE

LEADERS DON'T JUST have a job to do, they have a life to live. The aim of this Unit is to show you how your life is an essential part of your work for God.

What comes into your mind when you hear the word holiness? Elderly ladies with buns and black stockings? Hair shirts? Getting up at 4:00 o'clock in the morning? Stained glass windows? Fasting? Long prayer meetings? Holiness should never be a negative word for Christians. The Bible regards holiness as that delicious quality that marks out authentic Christians – especially authentic Christian leaders. It means being devoted to God and different from the world. It is living the life.

In the last Unit, we thought about the qualities God looks for in leaders. But it's one thing to show evidence of them at the start, how do we keep it up? How do we live the life under the pressure of leadership?

Here are some questions to think about…

1. If you went to Sunday School, think back to the people who taught you. Which do you remember most clearly – the things they said or the kind of people they were?

2. Whenever the latest political scandal breaks, we are asked to separate the private lives of our leaders from the way they perform their public duties. Why can't you make that kind of distinction in Christian leadership?

GET INTO THE BIBLE
Read 1 Timothy 6:11-21

There is a very special title used more than seventy times in the Old Testament to designate someone set apart for spiritual leadership – *man of God*. It is used of Moses (Deuteronomy 33:1), Samuel (1 Samuel 9:6), Elijah (1 Kings 17:18) and David (Nehemiah 12:24). It's used just twice in the New Testament – on both occasions by Paul in his letters to Timothy. In this passage, he calls Timothy, *you, man of God*.

What marks out the Christian leader as a man of God? Here Paul exhorts Timothy to keep doing four things. The language he uses is active and forceful. There's nothing passive about living the life. . .

- **Flee.** There are times when running away is a mark of cowardice in the face of the enemy. But there are other occasions when it is a mark of wisdom and the means of victory. Joseph certainly didn't hang around in Potiphar's house when he was tempted by his wife.

  The word Paul uses means literally to separate yourself from something. What does he have in mind? All the things he has outlined in verses 3-10, including false teaching, a controversial spirit and an unhealthy pre-occupation with material possessions.

- **Follow.** Separation is not meant to lead to isolation. And in verse 11b Paul lists some of the qualities Timothy needs to cultivate in his own life – godliness that will shape the kind of man he becomes. . . faithfulness that will make him a man others can depend on. . . love that will seek to serve others without considering the cost to himself. . . patience that will help him stick to the task even when the going gets tough. . . the gentleness that will come from keeping himself firmly under control.

- **Fight.** Paul's word has given birth to our word agonise. In his day, it was applied both to athletes and soldiers – people giving everything to gain the victory. Paul brings these two thoughts together in a word of testimony towards the end of his life – I have fought the good fight, I have finished the race.

- **Form.** God had committed the truth of the gospel to Paul (1:11) and Paul has committed it to Timothy. Now it is Timothy's responsibility to form a team of well-taught men and women who will be able to pass the apostolic message on to others who, in turn, will continue to pass it on (2 Timothy 2:2). Men and women of God. . . Christian leaders are stewards of the doctrines of the faith. God expects us to pass the gospel on intact to others.

It's a tall order. Can Paul be serious? Go back to verses 13-14 – in the sight of God, he charges Timothy to keep it up to the end, just as the Lord Jesus himself did. What influences will help him to live the life?

Read 2 Timothy 3:16-17

This is the second occasion on which Paul uses the man of God image. This time, he speaks of the whole purpose behind God giving us the Bible: to equip the Christian leader (and every Christian) for all that life throws at us.

The leader's inner life must be nourished by a consistent prayer life... by disciplined time with God, feeding ourselves and growing in our own relationship with him.

THINK IT THROUGH

1. Look back to Question 2 on the first page of this Unit. Does this mean that every part of the leader's life is open to inspection? Is he/she entitled to any kind of private life?
2. How does genuine holiness differ from being holier-than-thou?
3. Someone once wrote this – I believe the Lord has taught me this lesson above all: never undertake more Christian work than can be covered in believing prayer... To fail here is to act not in faith but in presumption. How would you work that out in your own personal experience. And what do you intend doing about it?
4. Brainstorm as a group on how you can encourage more prayer for your leaders.

FOLLOW IT UP...

1. Read Hebrews 13:7. Think how much you owe to those who have modelled the Christian life for you and, if you can, let them know how much you appreciate them.
2. Ask your tutor or one of your church leaders to recommend the biography of a man or woman of God who will help inspire you to live the life.

KEEPING THE BALANCE

THIS UNIT AIMS to help you discover some of the priorities that need to be established when you are in a position of Christian leadership. Although many of the conflicting pressures will apply particularly to existing pastors and elders, every leader needs to work out how to keep the balance for themselves. If many of us were trucks, we would have been pulled off the road long ago for being overloaded. We are often tempted to think of our secular job as a necessary evil rather than an opportunity to glorify God. We may well have a wife or a husband and family responsibilities. With our local church ministry, neighbours and colleagues to get to know, a home to clean and maintain, we may wonder where we are going to get the time to do the ironing or cut the grass, let alone have a quiet time. And it only makes matters worse when we remember that, as leaders, our lives are meant to be models for others to follow.

We wish we could tell you that the next few pages would solve all your problems. Work through this Unit and never again will you feel like an exhausted plate-spinner surrounded by sticks and broken china.

You can be the model parent, employee of the year, win an award in House and Garden and start a spiritual revival. We can but dream. The best we can do is to keep our lives under review before our God, the spouse he has given us, if we are married, and one or two close friends. We can also pass on a few helpful tips to each other.

Jesus, as always, is our Master and Model. He knew what it was to be busy – on occasions, so busy there was no time to eat (Mark 3:20). He viewed the twelve hours presented by each day as quite adequate to do the will of God (John 11:9). Yet there were times even in his life when he needed extra time to spend with his Heavenly Father (Mark 1:35).

No one can do everything. The old philosopher put it well, 'If you can do this, you can't do that'.

1. How does this maxim apply to your ministry?
2. Brainstorm on ways of establishing gospel priorities for your ministry.

GET INTO THE BIBLE

Read 1 Timothy 3:1-7 and 4:8-16

The following star diagram identifies our major relationships and responsibilities. Paul is writing to Pastor Timothy about elders and deacons. It may be helpful, with the Good News Bible, to call elders, 'church leaders' and deacons, 'church helpers', as both are ordinary Greek words meaning 'foremen' and 'servants' respectively. In the church of God, great care is needed when selecting those who exercise responsibility (3:14-15).

The Leader's Responsibilities in 1 Timothy

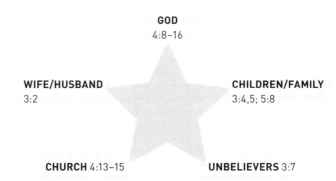

Let's take each point of the star in turn, with the references given in the diagram.

YOUR RESPONSIBILITIES TO GOD (4:8-16)

In our culture, tremendous emphasis is put on physical fitness. For the Christian leader, our spiritual health is even more important. This is the linchpin that keeps our lives together and fruitful in our service of God, so we need to keep space to cultivate our relationship with him. Remember, no pain; no gain.

THINK IT THROUGH

1. The analogy with physical fitness suggests that maintaining our walk with God involves effort – what elements are involved in training ourselves to be godly?

2. How can we keep up our 'hope in the living God, who is the Saviour' (v10)?

3. Why is it so easy to neglect this fundamental relationship?

YOUR RESPONSIBILITIES TO YOUR HUSBAND OR WIFE (3:2)

First on Paul's list of items for church leaders is the health of their marriage. Paul recognises that those who are married have a responsibility to their spouse which will sometimes cut into the time they need for their ministry (1 Corinthians 7:32-34). This relationship is that important!

Sometimes we need to say to married couples in ministry, 'Do yourselves a favour. Make each other happy. Have fun. Go out. Pray. Make love. Give presents'. Good marriages make us secure and strong to serve God.

THINK IT THROUGH

1. Does a leader have to be married? What are the respective advantages of being single and being married?

2. Are there ways in which your spouse could legitimately feel aggrieved that s/he is at the bottom of your priority list? Are there ways that s/he is treated worse than anyone else?

3. How can you put more in to your marriage and give more to your spouse?

4. Brainstorm on ways to protect your family and still make your home more hospitable.

TIPS

• Create time with God by taking yourself off somewhere quiet some meal times to pray. If each meal lasts about an hour with preparation and clearing up, can you use that time to foster your friendship with God? But remember – meals are important times for the family, so keep the balance.

• Save a few days of annual leave and go out walking with your spouse– catch up.

• Do something different that your child would really like to do – even if you draw the line at taking him to see Arsenal.

YOUR RESPONSIBILITIES TO YOUR CHILDREN/FAMILY (3:4-5; 5:8)

While there will always be conflicting demands in a fallen world, it is clear that you are not to neglect your own family to look after God's. There are times when you will need to refuse to answer the telephone to play with the kids... to go to the parents' evening rather than make the start of a leaders' meeting. Church leadership teams need wisdom in assigning ministries to those with young families. Especially as many people drop out of active ministry at this stage in life and never fully recover their zeal for the Lord.

THINK IT THROUGH

1. Are there any signs that your children are feeling neglected, especially in terms of indiscipline, which is the issue Paul singles out here? Do they have grounds to feel that way?
2. What could you do to help your bonding with each one? Brainstorm for ideas.
3. You've set aside Saturday afternoon to take your son fishing. On Friday night, the Pastor phones to tell you about an emergency leaders' meeting the next afternoon. What should you do?

YOUR RESPONSIBILITIES TO YOUR CHURCH FAMILY AND MINISTRY (4:13-15)

Paul lays down some fundamental priorities for 'his son' Timothy. Your gifts and calling may not be the same as Timothy's but we all need to know what our calling and ministry is. If not, we will be pulled all over the place.

THINK IT THROUGH

1. What are you concentrating on in your own ministry?
2. Are you currently doing anything that is unnecessary or would be better done by someone else?
3. There is certainly a need for personal 'sober judgement' (Romans 12:3), but it isn't easy when it involves your own ministry. Who might give an honest appraisal of your gifting and ministry priorities? And what provision does your church make for that kind of assessment at present?

YOUR RESPONSIBILITIES TO UNBELIEVERS (3:7)

The story is told of a virtually empty bus in Leeds that shot past two passengers at a bus stop, one of whom happened to be the local MP. On making his complaint, he was told that the bus would have been late if it had stopped to pick up passengers. Sometimes we can neglect unbelievers because we're too busy running the church programme.

THINK IT THROUGH

1. Why is a good reputation with outsiders so important for Paul in his list of credentials for a church leader?

2. What can you do to mend a fence or build a bridge with a non-Christian? Be prepared to share your actions with the group next time you meet.

YOUR RESPONSIBILITIES TO YOURSELF (3:2-3; 4:8, 16 and 5:23)

Remember that the all-time Number Two Commandment is that we love our neighbour as ourselves. If we don't learn how to care for ourselves, we won't know how to care for anyone else.

What is the general tone of Paul's personal qualifications for an elder? When we are under pressure it's easy to 'lose it'– to snap, row, explode and even drink or become violent (Paul literally has in mind a bare-knuckle fighter in v 3). We need to pick up the early warning signs and seek God for the self-control of the Spirit-filled life. Paul is very concerned that Timothy doesn't let himself go – spiritually or physically.

THINK IT THROUGH

1. In which situations do you find 'gentleness' hardest?

2. Check 1 Timothy 4:8. Does your weekly routine include space for exercise?

3. How can we 'watch our life'? And 'our doctrine' (4:16)?

4. Share some of the pressure points in your ministry and any practical tips with your group or with some friends.

FOLLOW IT UP...

1. Arrange to engage in your most enjoyable or least detested form of physical exercise.

2. Under the direction of your tutor, talk to one or two of the leaders in your church about the way they keep the balance.

LEADING THE FLOCK

THIS UNIT AIMS to introduce you to the dynamics of New Testament leadership. What exactly is the leader's job?

 Leadership has been described as finding out which way people are going and walking in front of them. Why is that an inadequate way of looking at a church leader?

GET INTO THE BIBLE

 Read Ephesians 4:11-16

This passage relates to pastor-teachers but, whatever the level, spiritual leadership requires the twin gifts of shepherding and teaching. The ascended Christ gives his church leaders who can both pastor and teach God's people (v11). From this and other passages, Paul seems to ask four things of the leaders he appoints. He calls them to be. . .

- **Pastors or Shepherds.** Although the New Testament uses the word 'shepherd' sparingly as a title for leaders, the concept is common (Acts 20:28). Leaders with the shepherding gift desire to see the church full of loving, growing, healthy Christians.

 Brainstorm on the other qualities you would expect to see in a shepherd.

- **Teachers.** Good teaching always involves application to real-life. Teaching will...
  - illuminate the glory of God and lead us to worship
  - deepen our appreciation of God's character and grace
  - uncover our spiritual resources in Christ and lead us to find fresh hope and joy
  - focus on character development.

Whatever its direct focus, teaching will always be central in evangelical church life. We have seen already that an elder must be able to teach (UNIT 3. 2).

Discuss the emphasis Paul lays on teaching in...
• Titus' ministry in Crete (Titus 1:9) and
• his own ministry in Ephesus (Acts 20:20-21, 24-27).

Paul indicates that teaching deserves special honour (1 Timothy 5:17-18). In the early church where tent-making leadership is the norm, this stress is striking. It indicates that teaching and preaching are so important that those who give time to them ought to be supported financially – and well supported at that.

- **Enablers.** Very often the way we 'do' church produces overworked leaders trying to motivate under-developed members. This isn't a pattern that commends itself to Paul. In Ephesians 4:12 he tells us that pastor-teachers are given to prepare God's people for works of service. Every Christian has been given gifts and, in church, Paul calls the leaders to mobilise the rest of us for ministry. This idea will be explored more fully in Unit 7. Without this mobilisation and training, the church's potential can never be realised. And here lies the crucial role of the pastor-teacher.

   The function of enablers is not to do all the work themselves but to train others to fan out in varied spheres of service. What about your church? Is every member engaged in spiritual labour?

   Perhaps some are uncommitted and don't want to be involved; others may feel inadequate and ill-equipped for service. The leader's task is to challenge the first group and encourage the second. Either way, healthy churches cannot develop unless this discipleship process is encouraged.

   Enabling like this needs to be modelled – see UNIT 3.10 in this Track. No wonder Paul exhorts church leaders to exemplify the Christian life. He tells the Philippian Christians to join with others in following his example and take note of those who live according to his apostolic pattern (Philippians 3:17). He expects Timothy to be an example in speech, in life, in love, in faith and in purity (1 Timothy 4:12).

- **Overseers.** Again in his parting message to the Ephesian elders, Paul exhorts them to exercise not only their gifts of teaching and shepherding, but also the gift of oversight (Acts 20:28). Look again at 1 Timothy 3 – management skills score high on the list of qualifications laid out for elders.

   Of course, leadership is always open to abuse. Plurality of leaders is a safer pattern than power residing in the hands of one man, but even a group of leaders can become dictatorial. The New Testament teaches servant-leadership. Jesus warns his disciples against 'lording it' over people and constructing hierarchical management models that rely on position and power. However, servant-leadership does not mean the absence of authority, it means authority exercised in love and humility and with great patience in order to build up God's people.

Discuss the leadership-styles adopted by. . .
* *the Lord Jesus in the Upper Room (John 13) and*
* *the apostles in the Jerusalem church (Acts 6).*

THINK IT THROUGH

1. The best leaders are those other people want to follow. Brainstorm to produce a list of qualities you should look for in a good leader.

2. Think of three pastoral issues that a church leaders' meeting might confront today that would not have featured on the agenda twenty-five years ago.

3. Given the demands outlined so far in this Track, who can possibly be equal to a challenge like this? Think of some appropriate and inappropriate ways in which leaders might tackle their natural feelings of inadequacy?

4. Write down some of the advantages and disadvantages of setting goals in church life.

FOLLOW IT UP...

Find a friend and read Nehemiah Chapters 1–6. You'll discover the background in the Understanding the Bible Track, Unit 1. 3. Together, study his example as an Old Testament leader under these headings. . .
* *vision*
* *evaluation*
* *formulation (coming up with a plan)*
* *motivation*
* *organisation*
* *action*
* *completion*

WORKING WITH TEAMS

THIS UNIT AIMS to introduce you to the dynamics of team-working and how to master them. The FA Cup Final and the Wimbledon Tennis Finals have a lot in common – huge numbers of people spend large sums of money to watch mega-fit sporting celebrities performing at the peak of their game. But what are the differences between a singles match and a game of football? Which better illustrates the Christian life? As leaders or potential leaders, most of us will have to work in a team – whether it is an Eldership, Ladies' Meeting Committee or Christian Union Executive. There is potential for great blessing when the team works well (Psalm 133:1). But if it becomes divided, it can poison the whole work (1 Corinthians 3:1-4).

1. *Think of some of the Old Testament giants, like Elijah. Are they natural team players or rugged individualists?*
2. *Are the examples of the Lord Jesus and Paul different?*

GET INTO THE BIBLE

Read Acts 9:10-16

Why do you think the Lord involved Ananias in the restoration of Saul's sight?

Paul is a clearly a man of vision and action. He is, as Ananias is told, 'a chosen instrument' for a great mission. For daring, Paul often seems rather like the 'American dream' figure, Superman who swoops in to administer justice, single-handedly. But Paul is a leader not a lone-ranger, and leaders, by definition, have teams. So Paul always has men and women who work with him and on whom he depends (Romans 16).

Read Acts 13:1-3;15:36-16:10

1. *How do the early church and Paul go about identifying and building teams?*
2. *What are some of the problems that Paul's teams encounter?*
3. *Look at 2 Timothy 4:9-18 – are the outcomes positive or negative?*

Teams are great – but the old quip about a committee being a group that takes minutes and wastes hours is as potentially true today as ever. How do we make sure that leaders lead and people of vision are supported not strangled? From the passages see how Paul and his teams get the balance right.

People who study teams have identified a collective life cycle…

- **the forming stage,** all very exciting if a bit daunting
- **the storming stage,** where the agendas or assumptions of the various team members clash and there can be a feeling of unease. If the team comes through this it reaches…
- **the norming stage,** with defined aims and values and strong relationships, which at the optimum leads to…
- **the performing stage,** where no problem seems too big and there is no end in sight. But all good things do come to an end (at least in this life) and even if the team is not broken up by life events, it will move on to…
- **the platforming stage,** where inertia can set in and new blood or new impetus is required.

This scheme doesn't come from the pages of Scripture, but we can at least evaluate and learn from the research of others. It may be that teams that go on and on create a 'corks in bottles' syndrome where there is no opportunity for others to exercise and develop their gifts. We forget that we are all getting old! If you serve on any ministry teams, do you recognise where they are in this cycle?

God brings the leaders of the Antioch Church together for a particular reason at a particular time and they respond with vision and faith.

THINK IT THROUGH

1. Why is 'rugged individualism' not an appropriate style in church ministry?
2. Think of a team you're involved in at church. Where are you in the collective life cycle?
3. Why do you think God has brought your group together to serve him in his (local) church in this place and at this time?
4. Brainstorm...
   - what are the plus points of working in teams?
   - how can we move more teams towards the performing stage?
   - what can be done to revitalise the performance of the platforming team?

FOLLOW IT UP...

1. A speaker at a large Christian convention began his address to a group of missionaries home on furlough like this – 'What is your greatest problem as missionaries? It is not homesickness, medical problems, culture shock or the language barrier. Your biggest problem is working with your fellow missionaries.' Can he possibly have been right?
2. How can your own mix of gifts, personality traits and experiences be used to serve the team(s) in which you are involved? Chat through the issues with your tutor or a team leader in your church.

DEALING WITH PEOPLE

THIS UNIT IS DESIGNED to make you think about the challenge of caring for the people you may have to lead, warts and all. Remember the old rhyme?

> 'To dwell above with saints we love,
> That really will be glory.
> To dwell below with saints we know,
> Now that's another story.'

It's as well not to be too starry-eyed when we think about the church. The Bible often says we're just like sheep – stupid, smelly and prone to disease. Yet the truth is that these sheep are precious enough for God's own Son to pay for them with his blood. So we must handle them with great love and care... and never forget that church leaders themselves are simply sheep thinly disguised as shepherds.

'Handling people need not be so difficult. All you need is inexhaustible patience, unfailing insight, unshakeable nervous stability, an unbreakable will, decisive judgement, infrangible (resilient) physique, irrepressible spirit, plus unfeigned affection for all people and an awful lot of experience.'[1] That's very tongue-in-cheek. What's your experience of dealing with people?

GET INTO THE BIBLE

Read 1 Samuel 30

In this incident we see David at his best. Here is Jesus in David. David was a longtime training to be king. You can't hurry leadership. It started as a boy on the Judaean Hills with his dad's sheep around Bethlehem. Caring for sheep is pretty good preparation for caring for people.

Paul tells the leaders of the Ephesian church, 'Keep watch over yourselves and all the flock of which the Holy Spirit has made you overseers. Be shepherds of the church of God which he bought with his own blood.' (Acts 20:28)

ALL THE KING'S MEN

The next phase of David's in-service training for royalty is to lead a bunch of men from the margins of life in Israel – a real band on the run. What are these men like? You'll find the background in 1 Samuel 22:1-2.

For much of this time it's a question of survival. David does some dubious things, including attempting to deceive the Philistine King, Achish, in order to gain his patronage, becoming a Philistine Fifth Column. Achish grants him the city of Ziglag to act as a base. The other Philistine rulers are suspicious. They refuse to let David's private army join them in a military operation and insist that he is sent home (see 1 Samuel 27 and 29). They arrive back after a three-day march to a scene of total devastation. Ziglag is a bomb site. Their families are missing. No one knows where they are or even whether they are alive or dead. David's men are ready to stone him.

CRITICISM

If you are a leader, criticism goes with the territory. The saying 'If you can't stand the heat, get out of the pulpit' doesn't just apply to pastors.

The way we handle people when we are under pressure will determine the quality of our leadership. Even if no one else is encouraging us, we must know where to find encouragement and direction.

Someone has described the church as a family with a mission. Leaders are responsible for the achievement of tasks, which involves the management of teams which involves the treatment of individuals.

----

[1] Eric Webster, quoted in How To Close Your Church In A Decade, Cohen & Gaukroger, Scripture Union, p 156

INDIVIDUAL

Remember David is drained, physically and emotionally. He and his men have to carry all the food and drink they have. Someone finds a half-dead foreigner – a 'nobody'– in the open country and drags him over to David. How does David deal with an individual here (1 Samuel 30:11-16)?

TASK

A little phrase from the life of Gideon (Judges 8:4) describes the condition of David and his men in 1 Samuel 30 –'exhausted, yet keeping up the pursuit'. But some of them just can't go on. They make it down a valley slope to a small stream, take a long drink and crash. David and those who go on recover everything – and more. Which reminds us of the riches of Jesus as he wins the victory and passes it on to us (Mark 3:27;1 Corinthians 15:57).

What do we need to recognise when we are enjoying the sweet taste of success (vv 23-25)?

TEAM

It's so easy when you are tired to accuse others of not pulling their weight. But everybody has a different capacity and we need to recognise this.

How is David here like Jesus in his treatment of shattered, burdened people (Matthew 11:28-29)?

The brook is called Besor – which means 'good news' or gospel. David is a gospel leader. He operates on the principle of grace – not 'fairness'. The other thing that catches our eye about David here is the way in which he shares out the spoils with his friends back in Judah. Godly leaders give and share rather than help themselves.

How can we show grace to those under our leadership?

DAVID'S PROBLEM WITH WOMEN

David is not always such a model when dealing with the opposite sex. This seems to have been a problem area to him to his dying day (1 Kings 1:1-4). Before we rush in to condemn him, we have to recognise that most of us are not half as attractive to the opposite sex as he was, which may be something to thank God for! However, the church is littered with casualties in this area, so to think, 'It's not my problem' is foolish in the extreme.

Why do you think leaders can become targets for the opposite sex? Paul's advice to 'his son' Timothy puts it in a nutshell (1 Timothy 5:1-2).

THINK IT THROUGH

1. How does David react to personal crisis? To personal criticism? See verses 1-8.

2. What issues cause tension between leaders and teams? What about your own sphere of ministry?

3. As leaders what kind of things could we be trying to keep a tight hold on for ourselves rather than sharing around with others?

4. What is good (or poor) pastoral practice when it comes to ministry to/with the opposite sex?

5. In 1 Corinthians 13:4-7, Paul uses fifteen words to describe love. Examine how each facet of the diamond of love should determine the shape of our relationships.

FOLLOW IT UP...

1. Make a quick résumé of the leadership qualities David has demonstrated in 1 Samuel 30. How does he create trust, respect and loyalty from his men?

2. Should a leader have close personal friends in the church? What are the arguments for and against? Talk to your group or to other leaders in the church, find out what they think.

3. Two teachers in the Sunday School had an argument three weeks ago. Although they work in the same class, they are no longer talking to each other. You can cut the atmosphere with a knife. As the leader responsible for youth work, the pastor has asked you to sort the situation out. Discuss with someone at church what you would do. And bring back some answers to the next session.

MOBILISING THE MEMBERS

WHY ARE MANY CHURCHES like a game of football? Because there are twenty-two thousand spectators desperately in need of exercise watching twenty two players desperately in need of a rest. The biblical model of church is light years away from that amusing caricature. In God's blueprint, there are no spectators, everyone is a player with a vital role to play in fulfilling the game-plan.

The aim of this Unit is to open up the exciting possibility of mobilising every member of the Body of Christ where you are to use their gifts in the work of the gospel. There are many models of church. Here are two…

- **the one-man band** approach where the 'professional' does everything and the spectators cheer – or grumble – from the sidelines
- **the National Trust** approach where the emphasis is on conservation.

1. What are the relative strengths and weaknesses of these two models?
2. How would you characterise your own church?

RECOGNISING GIFTS

GET INTO THE BIBLE

Read Luke 19:11-27

1. What does Jesus teach us in this passage about our personal responsibility to use our gifts?

2. What does the failure to use a gift that we are aware of say about our relationship to our Father God?

3. 'I tell you that everyone who has will be given more...' sounds like a dodgy economic theory but understood in the light of Jesus' parable, it is an important spiritual principle. What does it teach?

4. Who controls the distribution of spiritual gifts? See Hebrews 2:4; 1 Corinthians 12:11 and Ephesians 4:7-13.

5. What do passages like Romans 12:4-6a and 1 Corinthians 12:4-11 tell us about the variety of gifts?

There is obviously a wide variety of abilities and skills in the church; how do we recognise them?

- the desire to do a job may indicate a gifting (1 Timothy 3:1)
- the ability to do a job normally indicates a gifting, though it may need to be trained, or even restrained at first
- the willingness to serve is a vital quality
- the opportunity to serve must be provided if gifts are to be discovered and developed.

The discovery and deployment of gifts needs to be undertaken in an atmosphere of love and honesty. Church leaders cannot allow the kind of free-for-all where all the church members do whatever takes their fancy.

THINK IT THROUGH

1. Does every member have a ministry? If so, what does this suggest about the nature of church life?

2. How do leaders get people involved?
   Match the three leaders on the left with the leadership qualities on the right...
   - *Joshua (6:1-21)*   • *enthusing*
   - *Nehemiah (2:11-20)*   • *risk-taking*
   - *Haggai (2:1-9)*   • *sharing a vision*

How do these qualities overlap?

THE IMPORTANCE OF DELEGATION

The famous evangelist Dwight L. Moody once said that he would rather get ten men to work than do the work of ten men.

GET INTO THE BIBLE

Read Exodus 18:13-26

There are four basic ingredients in the process of delegation…

- the transfer of authority
- the transfer of work
- the acceptance of responsibility
- the acceptance of accountability

WHAT ARE THE IMPLICATIONS?

Delegation implies that overall control has been retained by the leaders. They must keep an eye on the whole operation. The leaders must evaluate results, check trends and remain alert to developments.

Brainstorm on ways of reporting progress.

ARE YOU WILLING TO DELEGATE?

Delegation requires personal security, humility and common sense on the part of the leader. Moses is an immensely successful leader, yet he willingly accepts advice (v 24a). No wonder he is called, 'the meekest man…' (Numbers 12:3).

HOW DO YOU DELEGATE?

Which of these tasks could be delegated and which definitely should not be? Discuss and decide in your group…

- *routine tasks*
- *setting the vision for the church*
- *areas where the leader is not fully qualified*
- *team building*
- *discipling and developing others*
- *problem-solving tasks*
- *cases of church discipline*

SQUARE PEGS AND ROUND HOLES

Finding the right person for the job is the secret of good delegation. And one to which the Bible gives considerable attention. Look at Exodus 18 again…

1. What is Jethro's advice in v 21?

2. What advice do the apostles give in Acts 6:3?

3. Can you think of any situations where it would not be wise to delegate?

PROBLEMS IN DELEGATING

Don't delegate to people who aren't up to the job, whether the problem is due to lack of ability or lack of training. Delegation must always be related to the individual's ability to handle it. Look back over Jesus' parable in Luke 19…

- Give people small, short-term jobs first to let them prove themselves
- Be careful not to stifle creativity

Remember, delegation does not release the leader from overall responsibility.

THINK IT THROUGH

1. With the example of Moses in mind, brainstorm on the benefits of delegation, both for church leaders and church members.

2. We often fail to share problems in our ministries with our leaders. Why?

3. Discuss within your group how many of you have ever been encouraged to think about your spiritual gifts. Have you ever been invited to consider what role you would like to play in the work of the church? In what way has the awareness of your own gifts changed as this course has progressed?

4. In your group, draw up a simple questionnaire about spiritual ambitions, skills, preference etc. that you could use in church.

FOLLOW IT UP...

1. Under the direction of your tutor, talk to one of the leaders in your church. How have they been helped to assess their own spiritual gifts? (Be careful: they won't admit it, but church leaders can feel surprisingly insecure.)

2. What comes first in the culture of your church – vacancies to be filled? Or gifts to be used?

A DREAM

Imagine a church taught by spiritually gifted teachers… led by gifted leaders… added to by gifted evangelists… Cared for by those with gifts of encouragement, mercy and hospitality… funded by those with the gift of giving! But why should it remain a dream? That's the way God intends your church to be.

TIPS

- be encouraging and positive
- explain the benefits – to the church… to the individual etc.
- define the limits of responsibility
- allow adequate freedom of action
- provide for adequate feed-back and follow-up
- maintain trust and confidence
- stress the glory of God in all we do.

COPING WITH PRESSURE

IN JANUARY 1997, Hammersmith Bridge across the Thames was closed to traffic, causing chaos throughout the west of London. Why inflict such pain on the capital's already hard-pressed drivers? The bridge was in urgent need of repair. It had been built in 1827 to withstand enormous pressures. But traffic levels at the turn of the twenty-first century far exceed anything the original designers could possibly have anticipated. The result? The serious risk of a catastrophic breakdown. This Unit is designed to help you understand some of the pressures that are peculiar to Christians in leadership. Paul says that anyone who sets his heart on being an elder desires a noble task. But many who aspire to any kind of leadership do not realise that increased responsibility brings greater pressure. While all Christians face personal demands, leadership inevitably involves more pressures and temptations, some of which are peculiar to the role.

There are bound to be undue pressures in a fallen world. What particular factors may increase the pressure on those in Christian leadership?

GET INTO THE BIBLE

Read 2 Corinthians 6:3-10 and 11:23-29
(The whole epistle is relevant)

Acts records many of the Apostle Paul's adventures, but this passage reveals the darker side of his experiences. 'Forty lashes minus one' is the maximum punishment allowed under Jewish law – five times Paul has been judged and sentenced by the Jews for his activities as a Christian leader. In addition, he has often been imprisoned under Roman law and sometimes beaten with rods, an illegal punishment for a Roman citizen like Paul.

Few Christians in the West equal Paul in trials and tribulations.

 1. From these passages, what can we learn about...
- *his motivation?*
- *the extent of his suffering – which areas of his life are affected?*
- *the outcome in terms of spiritual growth?*

2. If this is Paul's apostolic CV, what does he choose to leave out? What are the lessons for us in the age of the Christian celebrity?

THE DANGERS AND TEMPTATIONS OF LEADERSHIP

All Christians will be subject to pressure in one form or another (1 Corinthians 10:13) but if the devil can cause a leader to fall, he has scored a greater victory, at least in publicity terms, than if an unknown Christian succumbs to temptation (Zechariah 13:7; Matthew 26:31).

Here are some of the potential pitfalls – match the danger on the left with the verse on the right in the chart below...

Danger	Verse(s)
Pride and ambition– every leader wants to do well, but the desire for the plaudits of our peers may overtake the desire to do God's will.	1 Timothy 1:3;4:1; 2 Timothy 1:13;4:3-5
Compromise with the world	1 Thessalonians 4:3-8
Sex – we are all tempted in this way, but leaders are especially vulnerable. They are in the public eye, and often have close contact with the opposite sex.	Proverbs 16:18-19; Isaiah 57:15
Jealousy or envy	2 Corinthians 8 & 9; I Timothy 6:10
Money – financial pressure can sometimes lead to obsession with money. Seek to be above reproach in this area. And always set an example in giving.	1 Samuel 18:1-9
Neglecting our own spiritual life– one of the greatest dangers is the neglect of personal prayer and devotional Bible reading. We are only as useful as we are spiritual.	1 John 2:15-17; 2 Timothy 2:4
Compromise in doctrine	John 15:4-8

On the subject of sex, have another look at Titus 2:1-8.

1. Who was Titus to teach and who was he not to teach?
2. Why should men try to avoid counselling women alone and vice versa. Check back over UNIT 3.7.

HOW TO COPE WITH THE PRESSURES OF LEADERSHIP EXPECTATIONS

The people we lead have a right to expect certain standards from us. But we must always remember that we serve God first, and his expectations must take precedence over all others. If we do our best as before him, no one has a right to expect more. When we learn to live and serve as in God's sight, then we will be better placed to cope with what others may say or think.

In this connection it is vital that a leader gives sufficient time to his or her family. They are our prime 'sheep'. Someone once said, 'When I go to a church I look at the minister's wife, and if she looks as though she has been baptised in lemon juice I know there are problems!' Look back over UNIT 3.4 in this Track.

DISCOURAGEMENT

This is one of the devil's chief weapons. David learned to encourage himself in God (1 Samuel 30:6). Always remember that the church belongs to God not us (Acts 20:28) and he is sovereign (Daniel 4:34-35).

LONELINESS

Happy is the man who has a good wife –and the woman who has a good husband. But a leader also needs someone of the same sex with whom they can share their problems, and who will pray with and for them (Ecclesiastes 4:9-10, 12). Paul did not work alone.

FATIGUE

Fatigue and stress are a normal part of life, but if either become excessive they will greatly impair efficiency and may even lead to breakdown. Here are some tips…

- make sure that you get enough sleep. Exercise regularly. And eat a balanced diet
- don't take on more than you can efficiently manage. Share the work. Learn to delegate (look back over UNIT 3. 8)
- develop a hobby or other means of relaxation as a safety-valve.

If in spite of these precautions the problem persists, see your doctor.

CRITICISM

All leaders attract criticism, it goes with the job. Moses was criticised… Paul was criticised… even our Lord was criticised. And he promised that it would be our experience too (Matthew 5:10-12). Our task is to ensure that our speech or actions are right in God's eyes, then we can endure the criticism of others.

However, we all make mistakes. As the saying goes, the man who never made a mistake never made anything. So we must always be ready to examine what others are saying and, if the criticism is valid, accept it graciously. We may have to change our plans, modify our methods, withdraw what we have said and, if necessary, apologise and make amends. Consult a neutral person on the matter. Then if we are satisfied that the criticism is misplaced, be prepared to stick to our guns in a gracious and loving way that reflects well on the Lord Jesus Christ.

DEPRESSION

According to the World Health Organisation, depression is set to become the world's most costly and debilitating condition by the year 2020.[2] Christians living in a fallen world may well suffer depression. Some of us are more prone than others. But all leaders face many of the factors that

[2] Quoted in The Briefing, Issue 192, p 9 Matthias Media

contribute to depression – burn-out, demoralisation, excessive demands, not looking after our own emotional needs.

What's the difference between feeling down and being depressed? At its simplest, when the feelings of darkness begin to impair the whole of your life. Symptoms may include

- anxiety
- sadness
- weight gain or loss
- loss of sleep
- inability to concentrate
- lack of motivation

Rest, a break from work, prayer, meditation on the Scriptures, and sharing the problem with a sympathetic, prayerful friend will help overcome the low times, but clinical depression itself needs medical help. Most people suffering from depression can either be cured or helped to make a significant recovery if they receive specialist help. In all of these matters, the support of strong Christian friends is invaluable.

WHAT TO DO IN A CRISIS

Don't panic! It's okay to need help. If you are unable to cope yourself, seek help from one of your church leaders at once. In any case, call upon the Lord. He delights to help those in need, and his servants are close to his heart.

THINK IT THROUGH

Discuss in your group...

1. Where do you feel the pressure-points are in your own ministry?

2. What steps can you take to alleviate some of the pressures on the leaders in your church? Go on, you've got the Bible firmly on your side – see Hebrews 13:17.

3. Go back over the comments on criticism in this Unit. How should leaders seek to protect themselves against becoming insensitive?

FOLLOW IT UP...

1. Review the work you completed in UNIT 3. 4 in this Track, 'Keeping the Balance'.

2. Study Psalms 42 and 43 – try to identify the causes and the symptoms of the Psalmist's depression and his response to them.

3. Costly, committed Christianity didn't die out with the Apostle Paul. On 20 April 1999, two students wearing balaclavas burst in the Columbine High School, Littleton, Colorado and shot 13 people dead. Media coverage centred on the killers' hostility towards racial minorities and athletes. But there was another group the pair hated every bit as much, if not more. According to some accounts, eight Christians were shot that day. How willing are you to experience pain in your service for Jesus Christ?

GROWING MORE LEADERS

THIS UNIT AIMS to get you thinking about the responsibility of today's leaders to raise up the next generation of leaders for tomorrow. Who has the most difficult job? A brain surgeon? A trapeze artist who risks death with every leap? A nuclear physicist? Or an air traffic controller who has the safety of thousands of passengers in their hands? If the apostle Paul were alive today, he would probably reply that the Christian leader's job is the hardest. In any given week, they maybe called upon to act as psychologist, go-between, social worker, hospital chaplain, administrator, personnel manager and philosopher. But, above all, their task is to teach the Bible and model the Christian life for others to follow. You may not be in church leadership yourself, but it helps to understand the issues. Many of the principles outlined in this Unit apply to every kind of Christian ministry. Ask yourself these questions…

1. Which adjectives best describe the culture of growing leaders in your church?
2. What is the philosophy of ministry in your church? Are jobs seen as opportunities for service and spiritual growth or as life-sentences?
3. If a couple of Sunday School teachers were to retire this month, how would the church set about replacing them?

Refresh your memory by looking back over the material in UNIT 3. 1. Moses had Joshua, Elijah had Elisha, Jesus had his disciples, and Paul had Timothy. Every generation needs a new crop of leaders. Ideally, the regular preaching, teaching and service in the church will help to prepare the next generation. But it is important to specifically identify and train new leaders.

GET INTO THE BIBLE

Check out the following passages.
What do you learn about raising a new generation?
• Exodus 24:13 and 33:11. Compare Joshua 1:1-9.
• 1 Kings 19:16 and 2 Kings 2:1-15.
• Mark 3:14 and Luke 6:13.

HOW TO IDENTIFY POTENTIAL LEADERS

Warning! Those who push themselves forward are not necessarily the right people to serve as leaders. They may be aggressive control-freaks. Virtually all the great leaders in the Bible were at first very unwilling to serve, or at least had to be specifically chosen and called.

1. What do you learn from the following examples?
   • Moses in Exodus 3 and 4
   • Gideon in Judges 6:11-35
   • Isaiah in Isaiah 6:1-8
   • Jeremiah in Jeremiah 1:4-10
   • Paul in 1 Timothy 1:12-14
2. In order to identify potential leaders we need to look at their character and other qualities. See how leaders are chosen in the following Scriptures...
   • judges – Exodus 18:21
   • relief coordinators – Acts 6:3
   • elders and deacons – 1 Timothy 3:1-13

THE SHEPHERD MODEL

One of the most frequently used models in the Bible is that of the shepherd. This is found in both Old and New Testaments. In the Old Testament leaders are frequently called shepherds and this is one of the designations assigned to the Lord himself (Psalm 23). In the New Testament, he is described as the Great Shepherd (Hebrews 13:20) and the Chief Shepherd

(1 Peter 5:4). He calls himself the Good Shepherd (John 10:11).

Read John 10

In John 10, Jesus expands on this theme, giving characteristics of the good shepherd which all leaders would do well to emulate. Study John 10:1-16 and 27-30; what characteristics of good leadership do you find here?

So a shepherd looks after sheep, tends them, cares for them, protects them, feeds them, and is committed to their good. The kind of trust involved cannot be taken for granted, it must be earned. It springs out of relationship. To build this relationship we must spend time with people – learn to love them, care for them, listen to them, pray for them. See Proverbs 27:23.

In the East a shepherd leads the flock, he does not drive them. He says, 'Come on' not 'Go on'. Following is a voluntary matter, it requires confidence, trust, security and mutual recognition. To change the analogy, at no point is a river higher than its source. Followers will only be what their leaders are.

LEADING BY EXAMPLE: MODELLING
THE BIBLICAL BASIS OF MODELLING

Paul often refers to this matter of example, and uses several words in doing so. There is the Greek verb, usually translated to *imitate* (from which we get our word *mimic*) and its corresponding noun, *imitators* plus a related word meaning *example*. There is another word, from which we get our word *type*, which means *pattern* or *example*. Peter also refers to example.

1. These Scriptures show how prominent this theme is in the New Testament. Pick out some of the key ideas in Paul's mind...
   • 1 Corinthians 4:16;11:1
   • Philippians 3:17;4:9
   • 1 Thessalonians 1:6-7
   • 2 Thessalonians 3:7-9
   • 1 Timothy 4:12, 15
2. The Lord Jesus Christ is the supreme example. What do you learn from....
   • John 13:15
   • 1 Peter 2:21?

WHAT IS INVOLVED?

In addition to teaching and example, training is required. This means imparting practical skills. As we discovered in UNIT 3.1, apprenticeship is a very ancient idea and usually involves a well-defined process.

Work through the list, putting the steps in the right order...
- *the apprentice does the task while the trainer watches. The trainer's role here is to be on hand to help, guide, instruct or correct.*
- *the apprentice does the job alone, but reports back to the trainer.*
- *the trainer does the task. We must be able to do what we are training others to do.*
- *the trainer does the task with the apprentice watching, observing and if necessary, asking questions. This process continues until the trainee is able to launch out on their own.*

TRAINING A NEW GENERATION: MENTORING
THE BIBLICAL BASIS FOR MENTORING

How else can anyone really learn what it means to be a disciple unless they see someone living out their discipleship? How can they learn what it means to live their lives under the gospel unless they see someone trying to do just that?

We are so accustomed to using the word *Christian* that we forget that it is a very rare term in the New Testament. The normal word for a follower of our Lord Jesus Christ is *disciple*. It occurs over 270 times, in most cases to describe followers of Christ. A disciple is someone who is being trained.

In the Great Commission of Matthew 28:19-20, there is just one imperative verb – *making disciples*. *Go(ing)… teaching…* and *baptizing…* are all participles dependent on the main verb, *to make disciples*. So often we are content to make *converts* or mere *decisions* when we should be making disciples, that is disciplined followers… those who are being trained. Discipling is another word for the more modern term, mentoring.

Moses mentored Joshua; Elijah mentored Elisha; Jesus mentored his disciples and Paul mentored Timothy. We fail to produce strong Christians when we stress making decisions for Christ rather than disciples of Christ.

COST-BENEFIT ANALYSIS

Brainstorm on the benefits and the costs of mentoring – both to the mentor and the mentored.

WE ARE NOT INDISPENSABLE

It is not enough to have success, we must also seek to have successors. Part of our existing job is to reproduce leaders to succeed us. We must be ready to serve, to help and to train others. And then we must be ready to step down and pass on the baton to others.

What are the dangers of...
- *handing over too quickly?*
- *hanging on too long?*

THINK IT THROUGH

1. Does your church operate a mentoring system? What would be involved to set one up?

2. What room is there in your fellowship for people to exercise their gifts?

3. Imagine you are mentoring a young Christian. Devise a plan for teaching them how to develop their daily Quiet Time.

FOLLOW IT UP...

1. If you had to relinquish the ministry God has given you at the moment, who do you think would be ready to take over?

2. Everyone should have an apprentice. Is there someone in the group you work with, or in the wider church fellowship you could draw alongside you to begin training along the lines suggested in this Unit? Under the direction of your tutor, talk to your church leaders to see what they think.

NOTES

Continue your studies at home with the
Open Bible Institute
— a thoroughly Bible-centred, distance-learning college

One of the great seats of learning

• **Short Courses in ministry skills:** 10-session courses in Administration, Christian Mission & Ministry, Pastoral Care, Preaching and Youth & Children's Work.

• **The Moore College Correspondence Course:** a great course encompassing biblical studies, church history, doctrine, apologetics and ethics.

• **Certificates of Higher Education:** fully validated qualifications in 'Biblical Studies and Theology' and 'Biblical Studies and Ministry' equivalent to the first year of a degree.

NOTES

BE PREPARED
to serve the LORD

Prepared for Service **provides a unique, part-time training opportunity for both men and women with a desire to serve the Lord Jesus Christ and his people, to be better equipped for works of service in local churches, their communities and the world.**

It aims to achieve this by:

- Offering an environment where gifts and abilities can be realistically assessed to help understand God's purpose for an individual's life

- Providing a biblically-based training resource to help individuals develop knowledge of God's word within the framework of academic study

- Giving practical and pastoral models helping individuals serve in ways that are appropriate to the contemporary world

- Providing teaching, pastoral care and practical experience for individuals with the support of their local churches

For Information Pack/Application Form, please contact:

PfS
PREPARED FOR SERVICE

The 'PfS' Administrators
25, Felton Road,
Poole, Dorset. BH14 0QR

Tel: 01202 738416
Email: pfs@fiec.org.uk
Web: www.fiec.org.uk

FIEC
Bible churches together

A Training Ministry of
The Fellowship of Independent Evangelical Churches

Could PfS fulfil your needs in serving the LORD?

NOTES

NOTES

NOTES

NOTES

NOTES

NOTES

NOTES

NOTES

NOTES

NOTES

NOTES

Certification

If you would like your work to be assessed by an independent organisation then please send a clearly named folder containing answers to all the exercises in the this book to the Open Bible Institute:

The Open Bible Institute
Elm House
37 Elm Road
New Malden
Surrey
KT3 3HB

A marking fee is payable. For full details please see the website:
www.open-bible-institute.org/learn2lead

Authors

Learn2Lead was developed by:
Brian Boley
Richard Underwood
Paul Mallard
Dr Ray Evans
Tim Saunders